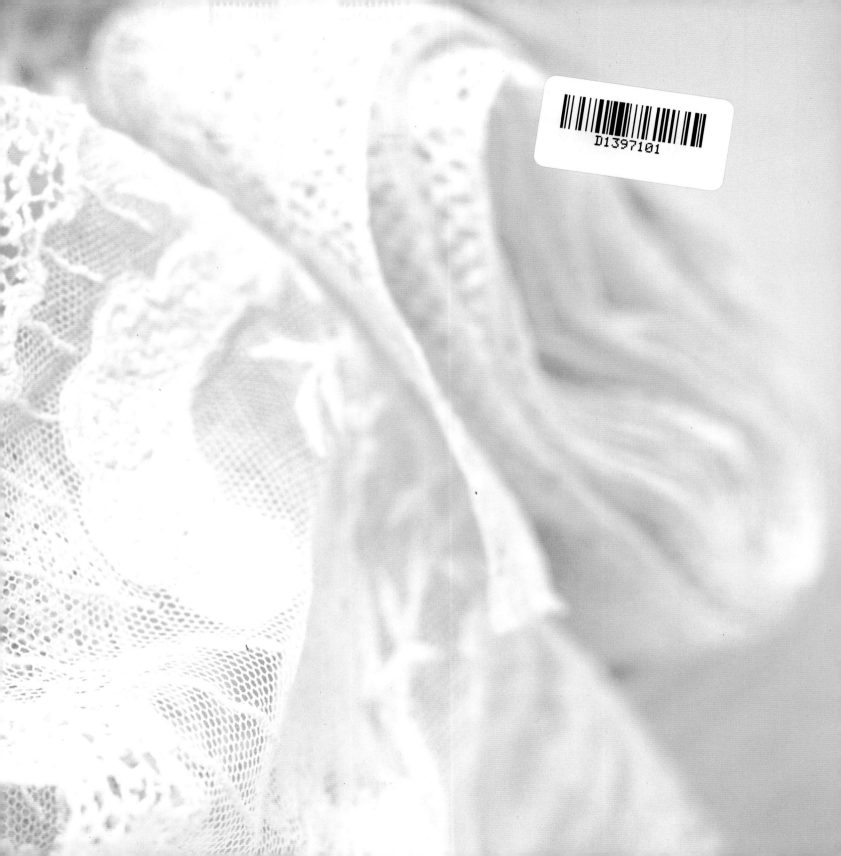

vintage treasures

vintage treasures

Jane Cassini & Ann Brownfield

photography by Caroline Arber

RYLAND
PETERS
& SMALL
LONDON NEW YORK

Designer Sarah Walden
Senior editor Clare Double
Senior designer Sally Powell
Location and picture research manager Kate Brunt
Location and picture researcher Emily Westlake
Production Deborah Wehner
Art director Gabriella Le Grazie
Publishing director Alison Starling

Text by Jane Cassini
Stylists Jane Cassini and Ann Brownfield

First published in the United States in 2002
by Ryland Peters & Small, Inc.
519 Broadway, 5th Floor
New York NY 10012

www.rylandpeters.com

ISBN 1 84172 287 1

Library of Congress Cataloging-in-Publication Data

Cassini, Jane.
   Vintage treasures : transforming flea market finds
   into decorations, keepsakes and gifts / by Jane
   Cassini & Ann Brownfield
       p. cm.
   Includes index.
   ISBN 1-84172-287-1
    1. Handicraft. 2. Recycling (Waste, etc.) 3. House
   furnishings. 4. Flea markets. 5. Collectibles in interior
   decoration. I. Brownfield, Ann. II. Title.

TT157 .C32 2002
745.5–dc21   2002024846

Printed and bound in China

contents

introduction

Vintage Treasures reveals the beauty and surpassing charm of vintage objects, fabrics, and ephemera, and shows how they can be adapted for the contemporary home. It tells you what materials to look for, where to find and how to use them. As you give your surroundings the individual stamp that only vintage can bring, you will develop a decorative style completely your own.

Vintage objects are intriguing—you might see a filigree brooch, a glass button, or a length of braid, and as you contemplate the design, the color, the shape and feel of a vintage item, you become part of its history. You wonder where it came from, imagine the people who once owned it. From an intricate piece of lace to a modest string of beads, the mystery and magic are indefinable, but undeniably there.

As this book shows, vintage objects can be displayed on their own or combined with modern materials to create a fusion that gives nostalgia a modern edge. Elegant, pretty, dramatic, or subtle—any of these qualities will emerge, depending on your selection and how you use the materials you find. Whether it is for a special gift or celebration, a stylish collection, or a stunning accessory for the home, the charisma of vintage shines through.

It crosses boundaries, spans eras, transcends fashions. When the craftsmanship of the past meets the design ideas of today, the result is *Vintage Treasures*.

Opposite Flowers made from delicate silk organza of old gold, mauve, and palest pink evoke the era of the vintage corsage.

Above left A charming handmade notebook, embellished with fragile glass buttons set within a cutout window, has a decorative handle of tiny gold and glass beads.

Above right A piece of Victorian silk, a twist of hat veil, and a necklace of copper beads—all pinned to a handwritten note—form an evocative collection of framed mementos.

Dreams of vintage—captured in intricate lace,
reflected in chandelier crystals, cultivated
in pearls within flowers, woven in elegant
embroidery—restore memories of things past
to inspire ideas for the future.

inspiration

Opposite A pinboard is the perfect way to view work in progress—it can be constantly updated, and holds everything from fabric remnants to tantalizing bric-à-brac: anything that fascinates and intrigues. Deep shelves contain a variety of vintage "finds," with hatboxes, bowls, vases, a filigree tray, and a jardinière making interesting containers.

Right Spools of hat trims and ribbon.

Far right A length of unusual braid studded with rhinestones. Behind it, buttons decorate the cover of a handmade sourcebook, which contains scraps of vintage materials.

Below A spray of metal oak leaves and hat trimmings entwined around a jardinière.

gathering

The dictionary defines vintage as "of high quality, especially from the past," and so vintage objects are of a certain age and style. If you find yourself gazing at a Venetian glass necklace, or a lustrous silver tassel, or a silk velvet ribbon, you could soon find your passing interest developing into a grand passion for all things vintage. Cast your net wide—with each new find, your collection will take shape, and your own style will evolve. How should you display your finds? A corner with deep shelving and a pinboard allows you to gather them within a changing display, ready to inspire ideas and to be reused in original ways. Here, a spool of silk ribbon and a sensuous pile of satins are a source of visual pleasure while they await a new role. A card of French buttons has already been cast as an *objet trouvé* in a picture frame.

This page Victorian and twentieth-century lace, and cards with lace trims; over an iron bed, a wedding dress with overskirts of embroidered net and silk flowers at the waist.

A checklist of vintage items to gather and collect would include beautiful buttons and buckles, sparkling rhinestones, spools of thread, silk flowers, remnants of fabric, ribbons and braid, old keys, tassels and trims, crystals from chandeliers, songsheets, manuscripts, faded photographs, feathers, illustrations…and ephemera such as postcards, labels, tickets, and theater programs. There are still plenty of these vintage items to be found, so get gathering!

Victorian and Edwardian lace is still commonly available, and even twentieth-century machine-embroidered net has charm. Be inspired by the lace displays in antique stores and use the ideas at home, piling it high on cut-metal trays, in wire jardinières and woven baskets. Pieces of vintage clothing, with their intricate designs and beautiful detailing, remind you of the exquisite workmanship of the past, deepening your appreciation and fueling your passion for vintage.

Gather elements from another era—luxurious lace, glamorous rhinestones, opulent embroidery —and begin an exciting journey of discovery.

This page A wrought-iron chair makes a dramatic backdrop for a stunning black velvet and ivory satin embroidered evening dress and a crêpe de chine blouse with a trim of rhinestones and seed pearls. Both pieces evoke the glamorous era of the 1930s. The embroidery and beading found in vintage clothes of the 1920s, 1930s, and 1940s often feature workmanship of exceptional beauty and quality. Whether you buy such garments in perfect condition to wear, or to make into an arresting display, they are a wonderful source of inspiration. Any pieces that are damaged or torn should also be rescued— they can be unpicked, and the salvaged beading, buttons, and trims kept for reuse.

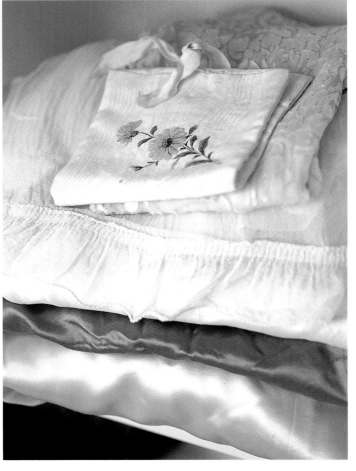

sources

To create your own vintage style, you must first assemble the ingredients. Where are they to be found? Sources of affordable treasures abound. They include antique markets, collectors' fairs, thrift shops, antique emporia, flea markets and bric-à-brac merchants, yard sales, and auctions. In a junk shop or antiquarian bookshop, you could find a fascinating photograph album or a shoebox full of amazing picture postcards. An old-fashioned notions counter might still have a stock of trims and accessories. A secondhand clothes store might yield fabrics from the past with intriguing names—cretonne, batiste, georgette, holland, sateen, or spangled chiffon. One of the beauties of

vintage is that whatever your style—elegant, exotic, or eccentric—you will find something that reflects it, so follow your own taste. It won't be long before you start recognizing the possibilities inherent in any piece. Fragments of grandeur should not be missed, nor the most modest trifles. Seen with the eye of the vintage enthusiast—who imagines things in creative and decorative contexts—any interesting object, complete or dismantled, scratched or damaged, has potential. Your search will be enthralling.

Left Period photograph albums give an evocative visual record of the past.

Below left A fragment from a grand chandelier, with its superb crystal pendants, is a fascinating find. Even a single pendant can make a beautiful decoration.

Below A metal wreath and pair of wrought-iron nineteenth-century plant-pot stands spill out from an antique store resplendent with chandeliers, candlesticks, and mirrors.

Intricate metalwork, a gilt mesh purse, porcelain roses—sources of inspiration from another age.

Far left and inset A wooden jardinière is festooned with a fantastically ornate French nineteenth-century painted metal wreath made of garlands of leaves, ferns, and enameled flowers.

Below A beautiful handpainted porcelain rose on a stem of gilded metal with oak leaves, formerly part of a garland. It is worth collecting broken fragments, especially when they are as lovely as this. They give inspiration and can be incorporated into other vintage compositions or simply displayed on their own.

When browsing, you might come across whole stores or stands full of intriguing items, so train your eye to isolate separate pieces and imagine how they could be used once you get them home. Nature has traditionally been a source of creative ideas and has inspired countless exquisite objects. Let it be your inspiration, too—delicate skeleton leaves can be dipped in plaster, or an oak leaf or seedhead painted gold. While exploring in stores and markets, you are not just looking for things to buy; you are also looking at the wonderful designs, colors, textures, and patinas of vintage materials—and as a result, your own source of inspiration and ideas is enriched.

Those all-important chance discoveries are often made where you least expect them—a long-forgotten evening bag in the attic, a wire basket in a friend's garden shed, a tin box in a yard sale. On a specific search, you will find wonderful clothing and accessories in vintage clothes stores, where the owners might be expert in their field and happy to share their knowledge with you. At collectors' fairs, where there is a concentration of beautiful material, you will glean all manner of fascinating information along with your finds. There is something of interest virtually everywhere. Remember, it is the combination of different eras, fashions, and styles, and the effortless mix of things that mysteriously seem to go together, that make vintage work.

Above In a London vintage clothes store, pearl necklaces, powder compacts, brooches, and buckles surround a fine collection of vintage bags from the 1920s, 1930s, and 1940s. The bags are in different materials: woven tapestry, embroidery, sequins, satin, and rhinestone mesh. Some have gilt chain handles.

Right A 1930's French circular rhinestone purse with gilt clasp, in pristine condition, epitomizes the high-quality workmanship of the time. This beautiful bag was probably crafted in Paris.

Clothing from the past provides a limitless source of possibilities for the home. Because vintage style is about recycling and reusing things in unexpected ways, it is worth looking at secondhand clothes that are torn or which at first sight seem unsuitable. They might contain beautiful trims or buttons that can be cut off and used to decorate table linen; the fabric, cut up, could become part of a fabulous pillow; a piece of brocade might be turned into a drawstring bag. Moreover, vintage materials look sensational combined with modern fabrics, so even remnants or small pieces are worth salvaging.

Above and far right The ravishing window display of this London antique clothes store features a fabulous array of vintage clothes and handbags. On an original 1940's shop-window dressmaker's dummy is a 1950's American Orlon beaded cardigan, still in beautiful condition. Cardigans like this will always be popular—the delicate beading can vary enormously from designs of spare, simple elegance to more intricate patterns covering the entire front. It is always worth looking out for damaged garments, which can be quite inexpensive, in order to salvage the beads and buttons, linings, and yarn. Just inside the window (above) is a selection of plastic handbags typical of the 1950s.

Above Among a display of white linen nightgowns is a beautiful Victorian cream hand-crocheted shawl draped over a dressmaker's dummy. Remember to keep a lookout for remnants of lace to reuse.

Right Still in its original box is a 1920's French beaded clutch bag. For the true collector, it is always highly desirable to find accessories in their original packaging, which adds to their value and usually means they will be in better condition. Beading like this can be inspirational—you could even make your own silk bag, perhaps in a much simpler way but still emulating the subtle colors and flower shapes of the original piece.

Below A Victorian cotton and lace camisole is displayed on a vintage dress stand.

Sublime tastes of the past conspire with those of the new—the glamour of vintage, at once simple and sumptuous, was born to intrigue.

There is poignancy in contemplating something that is beautifully made. You might imagine the person who crafted it, or picture the person who once owned and treasured it. An evening purse still containing a partly completed dance card with its accompanying tiny pencil reverberates with associations and meaning. In a sense, by rescuing old things, you become a recycler of human history. Sourcing vintage items is about translating the dreams and desires of another age into the present—and enjoying yourself in the process.

Right Splendid upholstery tassels of metallic or linen thread, along with some beautiful embroidered braids, were found in a street market and have many uses.

Far right A jumble of subtly hued industrial threads on original spools.

Below A soft fold of intricate lace.

discoveries

All that glitters is a potentially useful vintage discovery—a rhinestone buckle, for example, is charming, affordable, and versatile. But look beyond jewelry to less obvious things of the past (a spool of thread, a gilded glass button, a tassel); and beyond fashion itself to ephemera (postcards, sheet music, labels). A vintage discovery might not be of great monetary value, but once found and used with ingenuity, it can be transfigured into a thing of beauty. An ornate tassel from an epaulet, glass crystal beads from a broken necklace, a length of braid with detailed tooling—all can be reused in imaginative ways. Sometimes you will know at once how they are to be used, and other times the elegant context might have to await a serendipitous later discovery.

Right As this eclectic mix of brooches, clasps, bracelets, and necklaces shows, rhinestone costume jewelry comes in an astonishing range of styles. With starbursts, arcs, circles, and other geometric structures, these "fantasy" jewels emerged in the late 1920s, in the spirit of Art Deco style. Within the reach of everyone, and suddenly in vogue, they defined an entire period. A nineteenth-century paste clasp, also made of glass, glows more subtly. Both paste and rhinestone jewelry are essential vintage decorations.

Below Tiny buttons and beads are stored in a row of patisserie pans. In the background is an original hand-lettered sample card of miniature glass beads and buttons.

Opposite above left Beautiful glass "Bimini" buttons with their gold luster were made in London in the 1940s and 1950s. They were designed by an Austrian who lived in England and who is said to have been inspired by the shapes of some pebbles he found on the islands of Bimini, in the Bahamas.

Opposite above right Still on their original backing card are triangular mother-of-pearl dress buttons, probably of English origin.

Opposite below left A mixture of pearl and shell dress and coat buttons, some from Brazil, made between the 1930s and 1950s. Among the most beautiful of natural materials, pearl is drilled from seashells and freshwater shells from all over the world.

Opposite below right A selection of pressed-glass buttons from the 1920s and 1930s, and some cut-glass buttons on backing cards.

Left Silk millinery flowers from the 1930s and 1940s.

Below Victorian and twentieth-century lace in ivory and ecru.

Vintage inspires you to develop your own decorative style through discovering and reusing objects and fragments in new ways. Trust your instincts: through the process of discovery and selection, a personal style will emerge. As Cecil Beaton wrote, "Only the individual taste in the end can truly create style or fashion." If you turn a fragment of lace into a desirable gift bag, or a silk flower into a framed *objet trouvé*, your ideas are expressed and the charm of the object revealed. Beaton again: "The beauty of these things is somehow transmitted through the personality of the one who chooses. It is in our selection, after all, that we betray our deepest selves, and the individualist can make us see the objects of his choice with new eyes." By rediscovering vintage things, you extend their life and enable their inherent beauty to live on. "Without mystery," wrote Beaton, "magic disappears." In vintage, the element of mystery is ever-present. Where and when was it made? Who wore it? Vintage objects have a multilayered magic.

The design qualities of vintage objects and materials, and the manufacturing processes that made them, have passed into history, so in a real sense you are involved in a race against time. Each discovery is an act of rescue, of salvage. The sense of the unexpected, and the knowledge that something, somewhere, is waiting to be discovered, sustains the feeling of excitement. You do not always need to be out "buying." In your own home you will discover useful vintage items—a brooch from an aunt at the back of a drawer, or a clasp on a dress in the attic. Take time, and look at details. Your own history is important: there are rich discoveries to be made in a hoard of old photographs, or your relatives might have some unwanted mementos that you could use. What makes your vintage discoveries come alive is using them in a new context and combining them in original ways. Their inherent artistry inspires you to dream up your own decorative ideas—a cut-glass brooch adorns a cushion, a sepia photograph features in a collage, intertwined necklaces become a tieback for a curtain, an earring embellishes a fragment of mirror. And, in breathing new life into vintage materials, you create a link between past discoveries and present style.

Above An ornate Art Deco dress buckle with its ivy leaf and grape motif is surrounded by a stunning selection of Victorian and early twentieth-century buckles. These are all perfect for any decorative purpose. Even if they are broken, for example if the central bar is missing, they will still come in handy for display or embellishing a mirror.

Right A glittering array of brooches includes two rhinestone sprays typical of the 1950s. Such items can be picked up for a modest price, but have plenty of charm and make delightful decorations.

Far right A paste dress buckle gleams against a background of black and gold and a 1930's rhinestone and mesh purse.

There is magic in the serendipity of your vintage discoveries—with a little ingenuity, every find has decorative potential.

Above Draped around the neck of an elegant Art Deco-style gold mannequin is a beautiful 1940's Czechoslovakian rhinestone necklace set in brass.

Left On the glass shelves of a jeweler's shop window lies a 1950's cluster brooch with glass droplets. It is made of smoky cut glass and sprinkled with gold-colored stones that have a distinctive iridescent sparkle. It was probably worn on the lapel of a suit jacket.

home

There is tangible pleasure in using materials from the past. Imbued with memory and meaning, they help define a style that is truly your own.

This page Floral print, left; vintage necklaces of Venetian glass, pearls, and braided chains create a couture tieback (if the necklaces don't join at the back, extend with wire or ribbon), below; an underskirt of ivory cotton tulle, dotted with faceted copper buttons, bottom.

Right A confection of three layers of material—bitter chocolate duchesse satin, a flash of mauve organza, ivory cotton tulle—makes a fabulous curtain. A floral print of mauves and smoky grays, originally a 1950's dress, is made into a seat cover and cushion for a 1940's chair.

textiles

Remember the time of summer frocks and satin ballgowns, pretty scarves and starched handkerchiefs, flirty hats and the *essential* piece of jewelry…

The era of dressing up returns to your home, creating an understated glamour. The grandeur of a ballgown is reinterpreted in a billowing duchesse satin curtain with underskirts of tulle and organza, the "waist" encircled with a tieback formed from intertwined necklaces. Lovely afternoon frocks, too damaged or unsuitable to wear, are perfect for remodeling into cushions or pillows.

It is important to retain simplicity. Vintage style has an inherent beauty that needs space, so don't overclutter. In this way the spirit of vintage is enhanced. Creating an engaging mix of pieces that surprise yet go together, seeing potential in the plain and the ornate—this is all part of the pleasure of vintage style, which involves collecting and reusing objects and materials in unexpected, serendipitous ways. Stunning pieces of costume jewelry, originally worn to add emphasis to an outfit, now accent a velvet pillow, the cut glass contrasting with the soft velvet. Equally, a modest rhinestone button makes a statement when it is used to fasten a pillow cover.

A fusion of new velvets and vintage jewelry expresses the mood of the moment: nostalgia, modern-edged.

Opposite Distinctive pieces of costume jewelry have been chosen for their dramatic effect to accessorize a sumptuous pile of pillows. Pinned regally to each corner, glittering gems reflect the brilliant colors of the velvets, adding to the overall splendor.

Left Chic in its simplicity, a rhinestone button provides a sparkling touch to the back of a velvet pillow cover.

Above A classic 1950's cluster brooch of golden-colored and gray cut-glass stones, which would once have brightened the lapel of a simple tailored suit, now becomes the perfect adornment to a rich velvet throw pillow.

When pattern occurs in vintage materials, it is quirky, unexpected, beautiful. Vintage fabric patterns are often idiosyncratic, so they seem to recall a time when the artistry of the designer, or the skill of the embroiderer, still shone through. They retain an individuality that grows more enchanting with time. Look at fabric prints— delicate flowers of the 1940s, brazen florals of the 1950s, geometric inventions of the 1960s, psychedelic swirls of the 1970s—and you will see a whole era mirrored there. In your search for vintage materials, keep a lookout for scarves, remnants of fabric, and pieces of clothing, and imagine how they might be used, alone or combined with other fabrics.

When you come across a label inside an old garment, take a closer look. Usually machine-embroidered, often with immaculate stitching showing the name and even address of the design house, labels are time capsules from the past. Unpick them with care—not only are they fascinating in themselves, but they are valuable items that can be used in other contexts, for example on pillows, either singly or in rows.

Opposite above The geometric design of a chiffon scarf, loosely stitched to a velvet cushion, complements the lines of a 1950's Ernest Race steel and plywood Antelope chair. On one side is a small collection of other vintage scarves.

Opposite below A vintage dress label sewn onto a crisp linen pillow provides an intriguing detail.

This page Floral crêpe de chine from an old tea dress, lilac silk, and felted wool are pieced together to make pillow covers. A row of vintage dress and shirt labels decorates one panel.

Against an ocean of white, dreamy eau de nil, emerald, and aquamarine bring memories of summers past.

Opposite A cascade of pure white linen is caught at one side with casual elegance by a green spotted scarf. A café curtain provides privacy and diffuses light onto a medley of chairs, each with its own vintage touch.

Below A green and cream 1960's jacquard scarf becomes a jaunty tieback for the fresh linen curtain.

Right Embroidered and lace handkerchiefs, starched and hand-stitched together, make the prettiest café curtain. Choose only the finest linens and cottons, and keep all the handkerchiefs a similar size.

Rooms evolve as things are collected over time, and they change according to your mood or the season. One of the beauties of vintage style is its adaptability. Decorative ideas and color schemes can emerge from a vintage item that holds memories or catches your eye—a faded green and white skirt, an aquamarine and citron headscarf. You might remember another pretty scarf or some embroidered handkerchiefs tucked away in a drawer. Vintage materials mixed with crisp new linen give memories a tangible place in your home, and nostalgia a contemporary slant.

Yesterday's fashions—a summer skirt and a rose-patterned scarf—become today's home accessories.

Opposite Pillow covers, made from
an emerald and white summer skirt,
hold memories of the Paris street
market where the skirt was found.
The last sailboat button salvaged
from a childhood sundress finds
a safe harbor as a fastener for
the pillow cover.

This page Panels of floral fabric from
a vintage scarf and new aquamarine
linen are stitched together to make
a chair-back cover—a simple way to
unify an informal collection of chairs.

Opposite above Silk chiffon scarves of mauve, lilac, and cream form a softly ruched overlay when they are wrapped around a lampshade. Catch with a stitch where necessary.

Opposite below left A raffia hat with a grosgrain bow is sewn to a miniature lampshade, and a silk tulle veil is added beneath to hide the fixture.

Opposite below right Vintage hat-straw has been steamed and stiffened into a traditional shape and trimmed with an unusual flowered braid studded with rhinestones. To make the shade, an existing lampshade was removed from its frame to act as a template. The straw was cut and coated with liquid stiffener. When dry, it was steam-ironed flat, folded into a cone shape, stitched, hemmed, attached to the wire frame, then decorated.

Witty, flirty, frivolous shades of temptation—see vintage in a completely new light.

Left Part of an Edwardian organza and silk petticoat is gathered and attached to a length of grosgrain ribbon, then secured over an existing shade to create a romantic billowing effect.

Once you see how vintage fashion can be put to novel use in decorative lighting, you may never need to buy a mass-produced lampshade again. It is the immaculate detail that makes the difference. The picot edging of an Edwardian petticoat, the tailored bow of a 1950's hat, the sprinkling of rhinestones on flowered braid, the rolled edge of a chiffon scarf—all possess a quality and charm that shine through, and make light of your "work," which is to rediscover and reuse them in original ways.

So, loosely gather part of a silk petticoat, fashion a piece of hat-straw into a cone and edge with matching trim, use a hat with a bow, or enfold an existing shade in ice-cream-colored silk chiffon scarves. Echoing the elegance of the shades, heavy Italian engraved glass stands (circa 1930–1950) add a final translucent touch. These are just a handful of possibilities. As you discover more and more useful materials, you will begin to come up with plenty of ideas of your own.

Above A simple wreath formed from dried long-stemmed flowers, bent around and secured with wire. Oak leaves are added, and the wreath is then painted gold.

decorating walls

Dramatize walls and mantels with stylized wreaths, beautifully framed *objets trouvés*, and magical bejeweled mirrors.

Opposite Skeleton leaves and seedheads are wired to twigs bent in a wreath shape. Submerge in artists' plaster, remove, then leave to dry.

Above Photocopied book pages, cut into leaf shapes, are attached to a wire frame. Each leaf consists of two identical shapes folded lengthwise and glued together with a piece of jeweler's wire down the leaf fold. Leave enough excess wire to attach to the frame.

Usually associated with special occasions, wreaths can be a permanent form of decoration in their own right. Ideas can be gathered from intricate plasterwork, heroic laurel leaves, gilding, and from nature itself. Leaves and berries, twigs, and seedheads are transfigured into ornate plaster sculptures or gleaming gold metalwork when dipped in artists' plaster or coated with gilding paint. A distinctive paper wreath can be formed from the photocopied pages of an old novel. Ethereal or sculptural, these wreaths reflect the past and capture the spirit of today, enhancing any wall surface, distressed or plain.

Opposite main picture Mounted on ivory board in a frame of subtle charm, an operetta manuscript, a French theater program, a handwritten verse, a faded photograph, a remnant of hat veil, and other poignant fragments form a collage of evocative items.

Opposite details A Victorian metal hairpin with a postcard dated 31–12–23, an engraving pinned with copper ribbon, and a topaz filigree heart.

This page Framed *objets trouvés*: exuberant typography on a remnant of music manuscript, the frame draped with fragile strands of rhinestones; a music program; a 1930's hair comb decorated with ribbon and a gardenia of stiffened cotton.

Dazzled by rhinestones, enhanced with pearls, mirrors travel far beyond the functional, to provide sparkling counterpoint to any room.

Left A pearl earring adorns a pocket mirror inside a favorite purse.

Opposite Setting up a sequence of dazzling reflections, an earring is glued to etched glass from a Victorian photograph frame, and attached with fine strips of double-sided tape to a mirror. Beside it, a smaller mirror is decorated with a pin of glass droplets. Both mirrors are embellished with braid.

Details The pin looks elegant on a small mirror; an earring, signed "Robert," sparkles on the etched glass.

By finding and collecting interesting elements or fragments —a page from an old manuscript, a faded photograph, a lover's note, a ribbon, a brooch—you can create an evocative personal collage that exudes an understated beauty. Sympathetically framed, it can become a piece of decorative art. Search for things that are visually arresting, or that you find endearing, mysterious, fascinating. The collage is then a reflection of your memories and ideas; it expresses your taste, your daydreams, what you find moving. Even a single object, isolated and framed, can attain a dramatic beauty.

Mirrors reflect light, create space, and draw attention to a chosen feature. With pearls, crystals, and rhinestones, they become sparkling additions to the home and, once decorated, can be displayed singly or in a group. Where to begin? With the earring that has lost its companion, or the broken brooch that you cannot bring yourself to throw away, perhaps. So riffle through your jewelry boxes, browse around local markets, look for anything that gleams or reflects light. The older the mirror, the better the patina. If necessary, liberate it from an ugly or damaged frame.

Opposite Small oblong pieces cut from a broken mirror are dressed with rhinestone buckles and brooches salvaged from a bric-à-brac dealer.

Above A quartet of decorated mirrors is mounted on mat board using double-sided tape.

Right and below Displayed on a filigree picture stand is a mirror created from a larger piece of damaged mirror, embellished with an etched glass photograph frame and a pearl drop earring. Double-sided carpet tape secures the photo frame to the mirror, and the earring is glued on.

A glazier will cut a damaged mirror into smaller, equal-sized pieces, which can be decorated and displayed in sequence. Alternatively, an unprepossessing mirror can be given an "antique" beveled edge to give it more form. If etched glass removed from the front of a Victorian photograph frame is attached to a piece of mirror, an extra dimension emerges, reflecting and enhancing anything you enclose within it, such as a radiant jewel.

table decorations

Try a combination of crisp new linens and vintage trims and tassels, buttons and braids, to bring a sense of occasion to the dining table. With different shades, you can create a warm—or cool—sophistication.

From the fashion designs of Fortuny, Patou, and Chanel to the Scottish kilt and the English "uniform" of pleated skirt, twinset, and pearls, pleating and braiding have long featured in fashion and influenced the way we dress. Bring a dash of couture to the dining table with pleated table runners decorated with vintage braids and tassels. Matching napkins and accessories such as a gorgeous bonbon box, or personalized painted china, help achieve an inviting, intimate style that will charm your guests.

Mocha dominates the color scheme in this table setting, where soft candlelight is reflected in antique French gold-inlaid glass, and table linen is highlighted with metallic gold braid and intricate tassels of finely crafted detail. Center stage is an ornately decorated box softly lined with silk tulle and filled with golden bonbons.

Opposite and left A heavy linen table runner with a pleated decorated edge forms a dramatic backdrop to a romantic table set with gold-inlaid liqueur glasses and champagne coupe and a beautiful decorated box. The basic runner is a length of self-backed linen with the pleated edge made from a single, separate piece of linen. A length of rich metallic vintage braid hides the seam, with luxurious gold tassels and a tiny copper button providing a final flourish.

Above Chocolate-coated almonds, dusted with cocoa powder, are displayed in a *fin-de-siècle* champagne coupe.

Right Squares of linen are hemmed to make napkins, each with a faceted copper button at one corner.

Opposite A round box is covered with gold polyester "paper," used by dress manufacturers and theatrical costume makers. The pleated edges are formed as the paper is pinched, folded, and glued. The lid is decorated with a finely crocheted doily crowned with a silk and wire flower and a flamboyant tassel, and the box is loosely lined with silk tulle.

When visiting flea markets, always keep an eye open for vintage braids, buttons, tassels, and trims. Their intricate detail and craftsmanship act as foils to the crispness of new linen, adding depth and texture. Trims of gold and silver, once used to grace religious vestments and military regalia, are made from fine gold and other metal threads. While they are likely to be tarnished, which only adds to their authenticity and appeal, other items will benefit from a polish and emerge renewed. With the idea of bringing romantic charm to an intimate setting, and with your color theme

in mind—in this instance, mocha—look out for markings of gold and copper on antique wine glasses, plates, candlesticks, and other dining accessories. They do not have to match—an eclectic mix is beguiling. From a simple twist of old gold ribbon around a candlestick to the ornate trims decorating a candy box, the quintessence of vintage charm is captured. In this way—combining old with new, respecting the past, but turning it into something fresh and modern— an utterly individual style is achieved.

Rich mocha and burnished gold evoke an intimate ambience and the candlelit world of the belle époque.

Opposite and below A harmonious table setting shows the pleated edge of the runner with its vintage trims draped gracefully over the side of the table.

Right A leaf and curling frond decorate a plain white plate. Use porcelain and ceramic paint, following the manufacturer's instructions. Hand wash only.

Color has the power to transform a look, so the simple act of changing table linens and accessories from mocha and gold to ivory and silver brings a total mood change—from warm winter intimacy to cool summer sophistication. Forming the focal point for a dining table is an ivory linen runner ending in a procession of pleats. The cotton gimp braid that decorates the pleated edge is accented with cream linen tassels held in place by a striking diamond-shaped mother-of-pearl button. Plain white china can be given an individual touch by adding a hand-painted initial or leaf to each plate. Historically, the leaf is a recurring decorative motif, and initials were used by royalty and the aristocracy to personalize their china and commemorate important events.

Cool ivories and milky whites, lit by iridescent mother-of-pearl and silver, lend an air of insouciance to summer dining.

By adapting vintage materials and creating new contexts in which to see and use them, you are reinterpreting the past and putting a personal stamp not only on the objects themselves, but on your surroundings. With vintage "finds," it often happens that, rather than the decorative idea presenting itself first, it is the found object that gives rise to an idea about how or in what manner to use it. Thus it was with these trims and upholstery rings—first they were discovered in a remnant tray in a flea market; then later they inspired a use in a table setting. With this enticing mix of old and new, vintage treasures are transformed into stylish, contemporary additions to the home.

Right and above Ivory napkins made from squares of linen are folded and held in place by vintage cotton upholstery trims, which fasten like the belt of a raincoat. These pristine 1940s upholstery rings, perfectly matching the woven gimp, were discovered in a street market in their original unopened packaging.

Left A bold, swirling silver initial is hand-painted on a white plate.

plants and flowers

The appeal of silk organza flowers, fresh blooms, or a simple bunch of herbs is heightened by the subtle addition of pearls, jewels, and beads —delicate vintage dressing that extends into the yard with sepia or scripted labels and unusual planters.

Artificial flowers have long played a supporting role in fashion—from the modest sprays used for hat decoration in the nineteenth century to Madeleine Vionnet's magnificent chiffon rose ombrée of the 1930s, right up to the fantasy creations of today's couture designers, which signify, perhaps, a yearning for more romantic times. A corsage of fresh or fabric flowers typifies a time of elegance, when the smallest detail was all-important. With some effort and imagination, you can create your own, in vintage style. Translucent silk organza is ideal for the petals, while lustrous pearls give the stamens a touch of splendor. Alternatively, a real rose is enhanced when highlighted by a vintage glass button. Whether you are making a glorious corsage or a simple display, the aim is not to reproduce the real, but to capture the essence.

Center To create an artificial flower, make a stem by covering wire with double-sided tape. Bind with ribbon. Cut the petals from organza. Pinch each petal at its base, and glue them one by one to the stem to form the bloom. Make a calyx from organza-covered cardboard, and position at the flower's base. Stamens are made by wrapping tissue paper around wire, then adding a loop of pearls.

Above An organza corsage.

Left Ribbon-tied organza flowers in a slender vase.

Far left A 1920's mirrored button on one petal makes a rose into a fresh corsage.

A wild way to wrap a bouquet—with burlap and seagrass, root tendrils and vintage jewels.

Opposite The beautiful white blooms of (front to back) double lisianthus, calla lilies, and trachelium are swathed in burlap, tied with seagrass or root tendrils, and decorated with special pieces of vintage jewelry.

This page Tendrils of entwined dried root conceal a topaz pin, above left; a 1960s brushed gilt bracelet with emerald green cut-glass stones encircles the burlap, right; a knot of seagrass is complemented by a rhinestone brooch set in a fine metal "trellis," below left.

A stunning contrast of color and texture is created when the exquisite forms of fresh white flowers are framed in swathes of burlap or rough linen and secured with decorative ties of plaited seagrass or dark root tendrils. Scattered hints of topaz, emerald, and diamond reveal the discreet charm of the vintage jewel—a pinned brooch or an encircling bracelet. They bring a sense of the unexpected and reinforce the element of contrast. If delicate pieces of jewelry are chosen, perhaps with intricate metalwork and small cut-glass stones, they will enhance, not overpower, the beauty of the fresh blooms. Bejeweled, swathed, and tied—do the bouquets represent a personalized gift of flowers, or is this an imaginative way of presenting a piece of enchanting jewelry? They can be offered as both. They say it with flowers *and* with jewels.

Opposite A nostalgic scene: a hand-knitted drawstring bag, and a comfortable pillow with an embroidered vintage label sewn to one corner.

Above left Bundles of oregano, liquorice sticks, and lavender, tightly bound with copper wire. The wire is threaded with glass beads of mauve and topaz.

Above center Charming 1940's sepia photographs from a family album are photocopied and glued to gift labels, which are tied to handsewn burlap sacks filled with bulbs.

Above right A wire planter becomes a grand outdoor vase for a voluptuous late summer display of snowberries, green timothy grass, birch twigs, oak leaves, and china grass. Line a planter with moss, then conceal the container within.

Left A hand-lettered plant label provides an elegant touch to a lavender plant in a vintage Spanish tomato tray. A label holder is twisted into shape from galvanized wire brushed with copper paint.

home work

Paying bills, mending, and doing the laundry feel less of a chore with vintage style incorporated into your work space in functional fashion.

What could be more pertinent than books, manuscripts, and print as inspiration for a practical work space? Illustrations, quotations, book bindings, manuscripts, typography—all provide an inexhaustible supply of available imagery. Title pages can be used as lining for storage boxes. Lines of poetry and quotations can be rolled into scrolls or made into hanging labels for personalized stationery. A fashion illustration, mounted on board, is transformed into a timepiece by attaching a clock mechanism. Candle boxes stamped with identifying numbers, their lids fastened with buttons, are stacked and used as storage containers. Apothecaries' canisters are recycled as pen and brush holders.

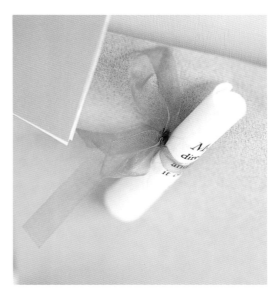

Opposite A profusion of items showing vintage at work.

This page A notepad made of old paper—the trim came from a roll of ribbon, top; a scroll of poetry tied with ribbon, above; paperweights made from seedheads and berries dipped in artists' plaster, with a coil of wire decorating each stem, left.

Right With the addition of linen-thread loops and shirt buttons from the 1920s, candle boxes exchange their utilitarian looks for self-confident style. Sew the buttons on, or catch a few threads through the holes and glue.

Below An old book with a secret storage compartment cut inside is decorated with a length of narrow ribbon.

Books, files, and ledgers can be covered in buff, cream, or ivory paper, reminiscent of parchment and vellum, and then hand-lettered in gold along their spines. A secret compartment cut from the pages of an old book is perfect for housing thumbtacks or paperclips, with the book cover forming the lid. Old wooden flatware trays are worth salvaging—they provide useful extra storage for pens, rulers, and office clutter. As an alternative to a shelf, a letter rack can be constructed out of plywood or composite and painted a subtle color. It will take up less room, can be propped or wall-hung, and will hold stationery and magazines in a coordinating display. For stationery, choose good-quality paper in fine shades: as well as cream and ivory, look at taupe, buff, and gray, and for interest add an accent color, perhaps mauve or lilac.

All kinds of office paraphernalia can be housed in clever containers with a stamp of vintage detail.

In these days of faxes and electronic mail, a handwritten letter is appreciated, especially if it is personalized by an apt quote or line of poetry. Search secondhand bookstores for the captivating covers of old paperbacks, novellas, antiquarian books, "penny editions," sheet music, or song sheets—all represent a limitless source of decorative ideas. Adapt, change, and put your discoveries to new use. With their distinctive craftsmanship and design, vintage finds have a way of retaining their original charm while adjusting extremely well to the modern world.

Above Sheet music from the 1900s is photocopied onto tissue paper and pinned with a gray velvet rosette.

Left Title pages and song sheets are used to line old stationery boxes, ideal for display and storage.

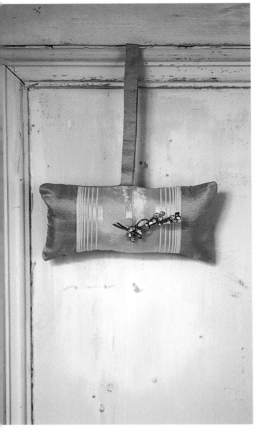

Above A pretty pincushion is hung on the back of a door near the sewing corner.

Right Elegant pincushions are made from new silk, trimmed with Victorian hat ribbon, and embellished with brooches and rhinestone pins. The pincushions are padded with kapok—in the past, sheep's wool, bran, iron filings, or even coffee grounds were used.

Old books on needlecraft reveal the astonishing range of skills once considered necessary for an accomplished needlewoman. They included pattern cutting, dressmaking, crochet, embroidery, appliqué, needlepoint, macramé, and tatting, as well as basic mending and darning. Specific advice abounds for the budding seamstress: "She should have a needlecase well stocked with a variety of ordinary needles—sharps and betweens—of different numbers. Then she should have a good supply of pins which may be kept in a small pin-box or cushion," advises one book from the

1930s. Needlework items can still be found on bric-à-brac stands and at collectors' fairs. You might find spools of linen thread, or tins with their original contents—needles, snaps, pins, hooks and eyes, buttons—all as useful now as they were then, and handy for sewing as well as craft projects.

This page A needlebook sewn from wool and lined with silk contains a pocket, a wool "booklet" for pins (not seen), and stitched inserts of cotton tape. A 1930's rhinestone button and a silver bullion loop provide the perfect fastening.

Opposite A quiet corner in which to sit and sew. The *Encyclopedia of Needlework* on the chair brims with excellent advice and is a pocket history of traditional skills.

Right A piece of brocade from the Edwardian era is lined with silk to make a bag. The drawstring is made by threading 1920's silk cord through Bakelite curtain rings.

Along with the useful advice in these old books is the acknowledgment that needlecraft is a creative and edifying activity—a notion that still applies today. So find a corner with a comfortable chair and, as a first step, for storing your tools, sew a few pretty needlework basics—a pincushion, a needlebook, and a drawstring bag (also known as a Dorothy bag). You can achieve practical and charming results by using beautiful pieces of vintage fabric, trimming with old ribbons and upholstery cords, and combining them with contemporary materials such as soft wools and opalescent slub silks. Look for quiet and restful colors: oyster, ecru, old gold, and greige—all suited to the contemplative nature of sewing by hand. Then there is the added pleasure of having a place to store your vintage sewing paraphernalia: quaint packs of needles, cards of darning threads, glass or mother-of-pearl buttons, spools of lustrous twist, wooden spools, a silver thimble. As the *Encyclopedia of Needlecraft* points out, "a practical knowledge of plain sewing enables one to appreciate other people's work at its true value."

Awash with vintage style—chic laundry accessories,
spotted and striped, in navy and white.

In the 1920s, Chanel launched navy and white as the coolest color combination, and it has remained a classic ever since. Spotted and striped navy and white fabrics give a pristine feel to the utility area. Headscarves and neckties are a good source, as are tickings, collarless shirts, rayon, and crêpe de chine from dresses and blouses. Incidentally, remember to retain the darts, buttons, and bows from vintage clothing, which can be incorporated elsewhere in decorative ways. After drycleaning, or hand-washing in gentle soapflakes, the fabrics are ready to emerge afresh as contemporary laundry accessories.

Above Linen covers for coat hangers have openings to take fragrant sprigs of lavender, with rayon ribbons attached for fastening.

Left Laundry bags fashioned from a 1940's striped blouse and a 1960's spotted scarf are backed with white linen, with neckties as drawstrings.

Opposite Navy and white bring a breath of fresh air to the utility area. A linen-covered box for toiletries is tied with a sash from a 1930's dress.

dressing table

The mood is romantic as you dress for the evening—
the story unfolds in silk, satin, and lace, and elegant
accessories take a starring role.

A jewelry roll is a boudoir basic, protecting necklaces, rings, and
bracelets. A roll of silk satin overlaid with embroidered net and
appliqués of rococo-style lace, fastened with ribbon and a dress
buckle, is the ultimate in glamour. For later: a taffeta silk evening purse
emblazoned with mirrored and gilded buttons. Fascinating fragments
from the past—silk satin from a torn slip, a remnant of lace, a dress
buckle, a handful of buttons—are reborn as today's vintage heirlooms.

Opposite A beautiful ensemble is softly reflected in
the mercury mirror on a carved wood console.

Right An evening purse of taffeta silk, with 1920's
buttons sewn in a cluster to form a bloom with a
fragile stem of seed pearls.

Below A jewelry roll made of softly padded silk satin
and overlaid with lace is fastened with ribbon slipped
through a 1920's rhinestone dress buckle.

collections

The need to collect and display objects is deep and instinctive. A faded photo, a postcard with a special message, a memento from a romantic vacation—such things hold memories and carry emotional resonance and, presented imaginatively, create a decorative personal record.

Opposite Vintage and contemporary materials combine to create handmade postcards, a straw bag, and a raffia travel journal—all nostalgic vacation essentials conjuring up the leisurely past of straw picture hats and folding cameras.

mementos

Vintage ephemera such as tickets and postcards hold vanishing imagery. By being discovered and reused in new ways, they are transformed into lasting mementos, and their fragile beauty lives on.

Above left White mat board is painted with bands of color, then overlaid with appealing ephemera to create unique handmade postcards.

Far left A notebook covered with modern raffia wall fabric and fastened with a striking hat ribbon becomes an original travel journal.

Left A bucket bag made from a circular piece of vintage hat-straw is painted with hat stiffener and steam-ironed into shape using a hat block to form the flat base. A 1920's silk upholstery cord is threaded through to form the strap.

Vivid memories of a vacation abroad—a favorite hotel, or a café on the square—are etched into a few stamps, a menu card, hotel stationery, a twist of ribbon, a tissue-paper wrapping. Transmitting their stored memories and associations, these mementos can be incorporated into handmade items—a raffia travel journal for notes and ephemera, or "scrap-art" postcards. Edited and pieced together like amusing mini-collages, they become souvenirs to keep or send to friends.

Left and below A beautifully handwritten card from Venice dated 17.1.28. A page from the album displaying vacation keepsakes includes a chromolithographed postcard, an Italian hotel's luggage label, and a painted silk image of a flag.

Postcards carry more than captivating images. Their stamps, postmarks, and graceful pen-and-ink messages give beguiling clues to other times.

Mementos and ephemera such as old postcards are saved for another generation when they are gathered and displayed in charming handmade albums. Fascinating and collectable, vintage postcards are redefined as art in an album setting. Covering an astonishing range of mood, subject matter, and printing method—from evocative sepia photographs to splendid chromolithographs and enchanting watercolors—picture postcards first appeared in the 1870s. Collecting them became a favorite pastime when handwriting was still an art. There is a poetic link between these old postcards with their penned thoughts and the albums with their windows into past worlds of framed memories.

Left and opposite Albums made from folded sheets of watercolor paper are bound with faded vintage ribbon. The covers have cutout windows, leading the eye in to postcards with exquisite calligraphy and an enchanting 1920's illustration.

Black-and-white photographs, secured with hatpins to an artist's canvas, become a mise en scène of images frozen in time.

From images of fashion to graphic reportage, black-and-white photography epitomizes "the caught moment"; with everything pared down to essentials, these images reveal the significance in the beautiful, the bizarre, or the commonplace. An artist's canvas makes a theatrical backdrop for a collection of photographic images; touches of glamour are added by securing pictures with vintage hatpins or using plumes and fake flowers. Smaller canvases can be painted in blocks of color, then decorated with a striking image and a corresponding brooch or clasp. Light-hearted and pretty, these canvases lend themselves to spontaneous additions and changes. They are a visual journal and a vision of an age, crisscrossing boundaries to form an exciting decorative focus.

Opposite A glamorous scene in monochrome: a pinboard is dressed with iconographic and personal photographs, hatpins, and fake flowers, while 1930's hatboxes with their idiosyncratic typography are stacked on a whimsical wire chair. The pinboard is a stretched canvas, backed with foamboard to secure the hatpins.

Above Vintage hatpins.

Left Small painted canvases hold a memorable black-and-white image and graphic piece of rhinestone: a 1960's "Paris" brooch, a 1920's crescent moon. Propped against them are the scrap-art postcards.

Opposite Precious mementos are grouped on an artist's canvas painted in muted tones.

This page A family photograph is pinned to a signed note with a sprig of fake flowers, left; another is placed on a fragment of parchment edged with gilt braid and decorated with frayed metallic gold ribbon, above.

A treasure trove of mementos is beautifully framed within a grid of soft painted squares on an artist's canvas. The grouping of seemingly random elements —a photograph, an embroidered letter, a title page—creates a series of narratives, becoming at once a personal archive and an avant-garde display. The tone of the composition can be romantic or poignant, witty or humorous. Intuition and a discerning eye are needed to edit and assemble the ingredients, and to decide what to keep in and what to leave out. Moreover, the composition need never be finished, but can change as the mood takes you.

A printer's type tray, painted the same color as the wall, seems to "float," and the compartments lend themselves perfectly to the framing of vintage finds. Isolated, yet part of a composition, each object is seen afresh: a rusty key, a French picture hook, some poster type. Empty compartments give a sense of new discoveries to be made.

These trays housed metal type for letterpress printing. Cases with equal-sized compartments housed capital letters; these were placed at an upper angle, so the letters became known as "upper-case." Cases with different-sized compartments were kept at a lower, more accessible angle, for "lower-case" letters, with the most commonly used in the larger compartments. When lithography replaced letterpress, type trays fell into disuse. Now they make apt showcases for vintage discoveries.

treasures

Recapture the childlike pleasures of collecting, and arrange your vintage treasures in a new setting to reveal their distinctive character.

This page A white-painted type tray hung on a pure white wall achieves a sculptural quality, emphasized by the intriguing mix of objects and deliberately bare spaces.

Opposite A French picture hook and accompanying bundle of nails, attached to the original backing card, left; poster type beside a Victorian buckle threaded with gold metal braid, right.

It is the links between the past associations of each treasure that give meaning. The inky sepia browns of the wood type "blocks" contrast with the paleness of the freshly painted printer's tray. Wood type, originally used in poster printing, can be coated with gilding paint, and used to make gold-streaked impressions on small rectangles of rough art paper. The original supplier's mounting card for an embossed brass picture hook contains beautifully crafted typography that could easily be overlooked, but is brought forward in a stylish setting. Other items that have no connection with the printer's world are chosen for their connotations or visual qualities: a gleam of blunt silver or gold, perhaps, or an accent of rhinestone.

A collection of imposing wood type can be transformed by paint into sculptural blocks of color, giving a change of scale and a clean contemporary look. With its power to alter the way objects are perceived, paint brings out the designs of the typefaces in greater relief and, lined up on a shelf at random, or spelling out a word, they make a striking display.

This page, top to bottom In a printer's type tray compartments: wood type, a rhinestone buckle, a Victorian heart pin.

Opposite above Obsolete wooden poster type is reused decoratively.

Opposite below The gold-streaked imprint of a letter A pierced with a hatpin made from a glass Bimini button.

Your search for vintage treasures is a personal quest, but the key to revealing their quiet beauty is to display them with simplicity.

Fashioned from various materials, buttons incorporated the innovative skills of master craftsmen, and at one time they were valued not only as functional fasteners but as ornamental miniature works of art. Theatrical or refined, ornate or simple, the button is a collectable item.

Vintage plastic, mother-of-pearl, and pressed-glass buttons shimmer on the squares of a painted chessboard.

Opposite and this page
A delightful array of vintage mother-of-pearl, glass Bimini, and plastic coat or jacket buttons find a new role as checkers on a gold- and oyster-painted plywood board, making an attractive display.

Most family homes used to have a button box, where buttons salvaged from discarded clothes were kept. The childhood memory of playing with a button box was one inspiration for this idea of using buttons on a handmade painted chessboard. The other was the chance discovery of some grooved molded plastic buttons, probably from a 1940's coat, which were reminiscent of checkers. Together with some opalescent vintage mother-of-pearl buttons, and Bimini buttons of hand-pressed glass with gold luster detailing, they make a beautiful collection. The colors are subtly reflected in the gold and oyster squares, which were painted in loose brushstrokes on a cream background.

celebrations

*This is where vintage becomes most fun—
where you can surprise and delight others,
while indulging your passion to the full.*

wrapping gifts

A gift bag of vintage lace and velvet becomes a gift in itself, and enhances the pleasure of giving and receiving.

Lace, that most romantic and evocative of textiles, first appeared in Venice in the sixteenth century and was once considered more valuable than gemstones. Exquisite wrapping makes the simplest of gifts alluring, and these gift bags show the intricate beauty of this vintage material to stunning effect. Yet they are so simple to make. Combine shades of cream and *café au lait* lace, the palest of tissue papers, rich velvet ribbons, and the prettiest buckles you can find.

Opposite and right These translucent lace bags with supporting tissue lining were made as gift bags to hold fragrant soaps. To make a gift bag, cut out equal-sized rectangles of lace and tissue paper. With the tissue on top, fold in half and machine-stitch the sides. Then turn inside out to form a bag, folding part of the top inward. Make a bow from a length of lace and handsew it to the bag. Thread a length of velvet ribbon through a buckle, and handsew it to the center of the bow.

Below Lustrous vintage ribbons threaded through a fascinating array of early molded plastic dress buckles from the 1930s to 1950s.

tea party

Relive childhood memories as you plan a children's tea party. Vintage picture books contain enchanting lettering for invitations, quixotic illustrations for decorating cards and crackers, and whole pages to twist into gift cones.

Opposite A children's tea-party table laid with party cones, decorative crackers, and candy bags. Gauze bunting trimmed with vintage tassels is festive.

Above left Crackers are formed from crêpe paper and tissue wrapped around a cardboard tube, the twisted ends secured with vintage braid. Photocopy handmade cards for decorative labels.

Above right Illustrate cards by tracing and painting, or photocopying, a favorite animal character. Ribbons are slotted though cuts in the paper to decorate the animal illustration and party envelopes.

Vintage comics and children's picture books—in any language—can be collected for their simple, colorful imagery, and the childhood memories they evoke. Cartoons and illustrations of animals—bears, rabbits, cats, and of course dogs, such as the fox terrier—are perennial favorites with children, and will always provide comforting inspiration for birthday cards, party invitations, and crackers. The bold outline of an appealing animal can be photocopied, or traced and painted; and, for a jaunty touch, a strip of colored ribbon can be tied around its neck, as if it is wearing a scarf or a leash. This can be matched with a ribbon slotted through the flap of the party envelope. Look for brightly colored fabric remnants or old dresses in secondhand clothes stores —they are all useful for turning into ribbons and ties.

This page Candy bags are made from tissue paper, folded in half and stitched. Make pretty ribbons from vintage fabric and knot each end.

Opposite above Ribbon decorates a hand-lettered nametag.

Opposite below left Party invitations are made from five label shapes. "Invitation" is inscribed on the top card; name and address on the next couple; and time and place on the last two. Interleave with tissue paper cut to the same shape, and punch through for the ribbon.

Opposite below right Pages from an old Spanish lettering book are rolled into cones and secured with a spot of glue. Add an outer layer of tissue, twisting the end to form a seal.

Set the scene, vintage style, with ribboned nametags and picture-book party cones.

These days, no children's party would be complete without a party bag. One way to make party bags look fun and intriguing is to use original or photocopied pages from old comics and picture books. Roll them into cones, and fill them with little gifts. Another idea for writing invitations and nametags is to look at the quirky old-fashioned scripts in children's storybooks and copy their style. Candy bags tied with ribbon add a tempting vintage touch to the table.

the cocktail hour

A heady cocktail to instill a sparkling mood. Miniature fans,
silvered and gilded, balance in elegant coupes for champagne;
while fantasy masks, flirtatiously feathered, are adorned with
pendants of pearls and ties of silk ribbon.

Exotic Venetian masquerades and costume balls provide inspiration for an array of exquisite fans and teasing masks, which become sophisticated decorative accessories for a drinks party and tokens for the guests to keep. The translucent silver- and gold-striped tracing-paper fans—bound with fine embroidery bullion, and with a delicate hand-lettered name card suspended from each—personalize a collection of etched-glass champagne coupes, which are grouped in an empty picture frame to bring the arrangement into focus. The masks, made from gold and silver board, are adorned with marcasite and pearl pendants, gilt and rhinestone jewelry, silk ribbons and swansdown feathers. Even the napkin rings are things of beauty—sewn from iridescent lilac silk, they are accented with sprays of sparkling rhinestones.

Opposite and below Arranged on a console table is a pretty collection of vintage champagne glasses. Each has a pleated striped fan, which is personalized with a guest's name on a hand-lettered card. Party masks cut from gold or silver board, embellished with ribbons, feathers, and jewels, add to the ambience.

Left These fans are created from rectangles of tracing paper striped with wax gilt, which is brushed between areas marked off with masking tape. Pleat into an accordion and bind at the base with bullion wire.
Above The napkin rings are lengths of lilac silk, folded and stitched, with rhinestone brooches pinned at the center.

Christmas

With an evocative mélange of the simple and the ornate, vintage style comes into its own at Christmas. Shadowy grays and browns unite with icy white to enhance the seasonal magic.

Beautiful old Christmas cards are a good source of traditional, nostalgic images, and they can be photocopied to make festive decorations. Dress the tree in vintage finery—silver bullion tassels, luminous chandelier crystals, glistening costume jewelry, anything that sparkles intensifies the magic. Under the tree is a tumble of bejeweled packages…and, on the mantelpiece, an angel, on tiptoe, in anticipation of the special day.

Above This angel, inspired by old-fashioned Dutch dolls, was made from modeling clay, painted, and dressed in silk tulle with tissue-paper overskirts flecked with silver and gold. The wings, tiara, and corsage were formed by threading vintage beads onto fine wire.

Left Vintage tree decorations and real candles, lighted or not, impart a magical ambience. (Keep lighted candles away from other decorations and never leave them unattended.) The vintage theme is beautifully extended to gifts, which are wrapped in pleated tissue paper adorned with buckles, ribbon, and jewelry, and to gift boxes, albums, and crackers decorated with wintry images.

Below A piece of fringed bullion braid is coiled to form a tassel and stitched in place. The top is encircled with rhinestones, and the hanging loop is made from fine wire.

Opposite right A resplendent 1940's earring with starry clusters of rhinestone and opaline stones is a perfect tree decoration.

Opposite Under the Christmas tree: a pile of presents is dressed with buckles and brooches, as well as pleats and vintage satin ribbon. Each gift box is carefully wrapped in tissue. Then a separate sheet, pleated lengthwise, is laid around the package and secured in place at the back.

Left and far left A rhinestone dress buckle; a starburst brooch of clear and amethyst cut-glass stones.

Below An old Austrian postcard is photocopied, mounted on board, and hand-lettered to form the album cover. Sheets of watercolour paper interlaced with glassine are folded in half to form the pages and the "spine." Thread ribbon through two punched holes at the side to secure cover and pages. Add a flat bow of matching ribbon.

A varied collection of dazzling rhinestones will add glamour and glitz to Christmas gifts, enhancing the individual charm of each stylishly pleated, beribboned parcel. A mix of tissue papers in evocative shades of white, gray, and brown echoes the seasonal color theme. Sheets of white tissue can be flecked with silver and gold paint for an iridescent shimmer. Encircling each package, pale vintage satin ribbons are slipped through a beautiful buckle, or pinned with an elegant brooch to create irresistible "fairytale" wrappings. And, to hold precious Christmas photographs, a handmade album, decorated at its edge with a vintage grosgrain ribbon tied in a chic 1950's bow, uses the sepia image from a postcard with its quintessential alpine snow scene.

Give a vintage twist to pleated paper, sparkling jewels, and a snowbound scene.

Old jewelry and bric-à-brac can be used to great effect when making graceful gift labels and greeting cards. Sparkling rhinestone and smoky marcasite, glass and mother-of-pearl, fine silver chains and filigree—these are all perfect ingredients for making ethereal vintage tableaux. Exuding a simple compelling charm, old trinkets, buckles, buttons, and clasps can be picked up for next to nothing in thrift shops, flea markets, or collectors' fairs. When a thoughtful selection is placed on a sheet of ivory or pure white watercolor paper, they take on an air of sophistication. Natural materials also work well. A little bundle of fragile twigs bound with gold or silver Indian wire bullion, with the addition of a single rhinestone and a handwritten tag (again placed on a sheet of watercolor paper), makes a beautiful card or a place card at the table. They are a joy to receive, and worth treasuring long afterward.

This page Fragile twigs bound with wire bullion, each with a slender handwritten tag, are glued to small cards made from watercolor paper. A single rhinestone adds a sparkling focal point.

Opposite right Paneled cards made from watercolor paper display a trio of sparkling finds. Silver chains encircle the folded spines, and each card has a tissue-paper insert.

Details opposite, top to bottom A rhinestone buckle with a scrap of ribbon; a marcasite earring; a knot of bullion wire; a marcasite button.

Piled up and waiting to be pulled, crackers add an important element of excitement to Christmas. Whether they hold a lovely gift or an amusing trinket, the childlike sense of anticipation is just the same. Crackers were invented by Tom Smith, a London confectioner who, in 1840, was inspired by the French style of wrapping bonbons in colored twists of paper. Borrowing the method for selling sugared almonds and other candy, he had the idea of tucking paper mottoes, or "kiss mottoes," inside the fancy colored wrappers. Later he added strips of paper coated with a

Vintage imagery brings a touch of nostalgia to decorative crackers.

tiny amount of explosive, to give the "cracking" sound when they were pulled—hence the name. Eventually, candy was omitted in favor of surprise gifts and paper hats, though of course the mottoes were retained.

Carry on this tradition by making your own crackers. For the decorative labels, use images photocopied from old postcards or Christmas cards. Choose cards with evocative illustrations, or photographs—tinted or sepia—that capture the spirit of Christmas. Either repeat the same image or pick different ones, and make photocopies in sepia or color, depending on the originals. The vintage labels gain a fresh, modern look when trimmed with gold and placed on crackers of pure white crêpe paper. Another essential at Christmas is the Advent calendar, which celebrates each December day up to Christmas with a little token.

This page and opposite For decorative crackers, place a gift and motto inside a cardboard tube. Wrap in a length of crêpe paper. Twist each end and secure with jeweler's wire. Using gold paper cake "ribbon," or the scalloped edges cut from doilies, add a border to each label and to the crackers' ends.

Above left A few fragile twigs of clematis or wisteria are bent into a wreath and sprinkled with single rhinestones.

Above center A little gold-edged card with a cutout brown-paper Christmas tree is crowned with a rhinestone "star."

Above right A dove cut from gilded paper, with pleated wings (made from a single piece of paper) slotted through its body, has a tiny bead for an eye.

Below left A golden spray of berries is created from vintage metal beads, mother-of-pearl leaves, and fine wire.

Below center A miniature cracker twisted from iridescent organza around a tiny cardboard tube carries a gleaming piece of bric-à-brac.

Below right A sprig of mistletoe is created from creamy pearls threaded through jeweler's wire and gold-painted leaves made from thin cardboard.

Opposite A beautiful vintage Advent calendar is made from an artist's stretched canvas backed with foamboard and edged with gold metallic braid. Twenty-four miniature festive tokens (one for each day before Christmas)—some found, some handmade—are attached to luggage labels, which are numbered in gold and pinned to the canvas.

Easter

Celebrating the arrival of spring, vintage silk flowers and leaf-green ribbons from an Easter bonnet make becoming decorations for an Easter breakfast.

An Easter celebration gets the lightest vintage touch. Floral hat trimmings from the 1930s—narcissi, lilies-of-the-valley, margaritas, daisies—encircle hand-lettered eggs in a garlanded centerpiece, and provide delicate decoration for painted eggs and a felted wool egg cozy.

This page A sprig of narcissus glued to a painted egg; a silk flower cuts a dash in the hatband of an egg cozy.

Opposite Symbols of spring: speckled eggs nesting in hat veil; beribboned chocolate bars; vintage flowers decorating a centerpiece of painted eggs.

Painted Easter eggs carry the message "Spring," in different languages—because, in any country, spring is the season of hope and renewal.

Easter has been called the Queen of Festivals, and it was considered lucky to wear a bright new piece of clothing. Traditionally, young girls and women wore a bonnet, embellished with flowers or ribbons of white, green, and yellow—colors symbolic of spring. Complemented by delicate white bone china, a gentle scene is set with vintage floral hat decorations of white blossoms and green foliage, and sumptuous 1930's sateen hat ribbon. With a diluted palette of almond green, primrose, duck's-egg blue, and chalk white for the painted eggs, spring is at once brought into the home.

Spring denotes the season of hope and renewal, so the centerpiece with encircling blossoms of white silk flowers contains painted eggs, with the word "Spring" hand-lettered in various languages—*Printemps, Frühling, Primavera, Spring, Vår*. Easter chocolate bars are stripped of their usual wrappings and given white paper sleeves, beautifully finished with green hat ribbons and chic paper bows—all within a table setting of silver and primrose teapots and fine bone china.

This page To prepare an egg for painting, pierce a hole in each end, making the hole in the broad end larger. Blow the contents out through the larger hole, and rinse through. Paint with latex and, when dry, apply lettering by hand. Sample pots of latex are ideal.

Opposite left Paper sleeves, bows, and vintage ribbon give chocolate bars a new style.

Opposite right The hand-lettering is reminiscent of the script iced onto traditional Easter eggs.

Valentine's Day

Romantic images and ephemera can inspire an intriguing Valentine card, while pearls and a corsage decorate heart-shaped boxes— creating love tokens that will be remembered far beyond February 14.

Give in to your romantic instincts when searching for Valentine inspirations in bric-à-brac stands. Look for illustrations of Cupid and Venus, trinkets of gold and silver, hearts lost from lockets, lovers' pins, tiny keys, delicate initials and numbers. Anything of pearl will come in useful—a bracelet or earring—and anything unexpected, such as filigree paper lace, or a rose corsage. Valentines first appeared in the fifteenth century as wood engravings. In the nineteenth century they became more sumptuous, with secret messages hidden from strict parents behind panels decorated with posies or feathers. Like their forerunners, vintage love tokens are best expressed in simple line drawings or woodcuts, and *trouvailles* discreetly presented within colors of tea and blush pink.

Opposite above Valentine-inspired images and ephemera decorate five rectangles cut from thin plywood or cardboard. Cryptic messages are added using letters cut from pamphlets or magazines. The five cards are joined together with a length of vintage ribbon, and close in an accordion fold. The ribbon ends tie in an elegant loose knot.

Opposite below Delicate filigree edging salvaged from a damaged Victorian card becomes the border for a piece of watercolor paper mounted on plywood. A silver heart pin and the message *Amour* complete the picture.

This page Heart-shaped confectionery boxes are painted in sugar-almond colors and decorated with pearls, a corsage, ribbons, and silk tulle—perfect for holding small gifts or love notes.

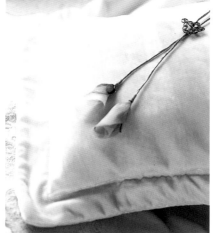

wedding keepsakes

Long after the day, memories are relived through keepsakes pinned to a wedding cushion and thoughts written in a guest book. So celebrate in true vintage fashion, for these tokens will be treasured forever.

Above and top Pale pink and old-gold organza flowers are pinned to a velvet wedding cushion with a filigree and paste brooch; draped over the French iron daybed is a stunning beaded and embroidered vintage wedding dress.

Right Ivory and pink velvet bracelets for the flowergirls are made from lengths of ribbon fastened with silk thread loops and shimmering glass buttons. A separate velvet strip holds a handmade organza bud in place on each bracelet.

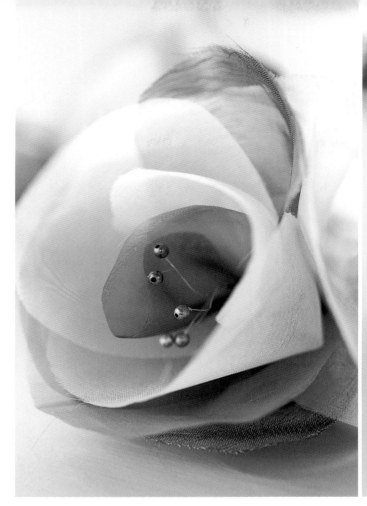

On such a special day, gloriously old-fashioned colors—dusty pink, ivory, old gold, so evocative of *fin-de-siècle* romance—join together with exquisite vintage details. Wedding favors to charm your guests are decorated with vintage ribbons, buttons, and beads, and will be treasured long afterward. Silk-lined rice or confetti boxes with luxurious bows overflow with tissue-paper petals of gold, pink, and ivory. Wonderful individual flowers can be created from silk organza in old gold and pink, some in full bloom, some in bud, and all elaborated with gold wire stamens studded with tiny gold seed pearls. Slender velvet bracelets, each adorned with a single organza bud and fastened with a delicate glass button, are perfect for the flowergirls, and become their lasting mementos of the day. Other flowers can be used for a bouquet or a corsage, or strewn over the wedding table to create a dreamy, theatrical effect, and to add to the romance of the occasion. Finally, as a tangible reminder of this momentous day, the bride takes two flowers and, with a cherished brooch, pins them to an ivory velvet wedding cushion.

Above left The flower petals are cut from organza, and a stem made from wire, covered with double-sided tape and bound with ribbon. The petals are folded around and glued to the stem, and the base finished with extra organza. Stamens of jeweler's wire are decorated with pearls.

Above right A basic box shape is cut from cardboard and lightly scored where necessary. The box is covered inside and out with silk, attached with spray adhesive. Once assembled, it is decorated with vintage ribbon and a silk cord handle to complete the prettiest rice or confetti holder.

An enchanting notebook for every guest holds sketches, photographs, messages, and new friends' telephone numbers—a useful reminder of a special wedding day.

Above and right For guest notebooks, small spiral-bound sketch pads are ideal. Replace the outside cover with watercolor paper. On top, paste a second sheet of paper in which a window has been cut, and place pretty vintage buttons in the frame. Glue a paper rectangle, edged with gold, to cover the spine. A string of vintage glass beads is threaded through the spine.

Above 'Sterling Silver' roses in a vase echo the old-fashioned colors of the wedding.

Right Invitations are made from rectangles of watercolor paper decorated at the bottom with a brushstroke of gilding paint. Use the same paint or a rollerball for the intertwined initials and, on the reverse, hand-script details of the wedding. Punch a hole at the top and thread with a string of gold and glass beads.

Weddings have a timeless quality, and the perennial beauty of vintage is utterly appropriate for the entire occasion—from the slender beaded wedding invitations hand-lettered in gold, with the entwined initials of bride and groom on one side and the wedding day details hand-scripted on the reverse, to exquisitely wrought handmade notebooks that help commemorate the day. Make a gift of a notebook to guests as they arrive, and have pens and pencils in small crystal vases so they can record their thoughts and memories, as well as the names and addresses of new friends. With each cover embellished in a subtly different way, with tiny vintage buttons and decorative handles of gold and glass beads, the notebooks will become mementos to be treasured and kept, with lasting sentimental value. Thus, with ingenuity and imagination, memorable things can be created from modest but charming ingredients.

new baby

Pearl buttons and buckles, cream lace and silky ribbons, and a nostalgic family photograph—the perfect combination to announce the birth of a new baby.

The most wonderful announcement, the birth of a baby, can also be a touching reminder of the past, of our own childhood, and of the future. A baby announcement is a chance to use vintage items such as a favorite family photograph, a button from a christening robe, and perhaps some baby-blue ribbon found in a flea market. Antique lace, admired throughout generations for its exquisite craftsmanship, makes lovely wrapping for a christening gift. To contrast with the texture of the lace, silky cream ribbon is tied around the gift and threaded through a tiny vintage baby buckle. Translucent sheets of glassine, normally used in photograph albums, are perfect for making large gift "envelopes," and an excellent way to wrap a special piece of baby's clothing so the gift can be glimpsed. Somewhere in your collection will be just the right mother-of-pearl button to sew onto the envelope with a loop of linen thread.

Opposite Inside an antique crib is a basket with a soft linen layette and a small gift wrapped in vintage lace. Over the side is a vintage embroidered net christening robe.

Above right A glassine envelope is decorated with a shell button and loops of linen thread. The end is left loose or wound around the button to fasten the package.

Below right A gift is wrapped in lace, tied with ribbon, and fastened by a delicate 1940's baby buckle.

No present is quite complete without beautiful gift wrapping, especially if the offering is a family heirloom such as a pretty, delicately hand-smocked baby dress which has been handed down from one generation to the next. The neat, pristine feel of a handmade box sets off the beauty of the gift within, while blue vintage ribbons, tied simply at each corner, give the container itself a period charm. The box is deep enough to hold several layers. Folded beneath the baby dress is a crisp linen layette and an antique lace christening robe, making a sumptuous mixture of fabrics, old and new.

For the baby announcement card, choose a special family photograph that captures a moment full of personal memories. With the addition of a fragment of vintage lace from a childhood dress at the edge, and a small pearl button tied with linen thread to fasten the card, the imagery is complete. Perhaps the card itself will one day become a treasured family heirloom.

This page A birth announcement is made from prints of a photograph mounted on board, and decorated with lace, thread, and button, above; the envelope is made from glassine. A pile of childhood books makes a gift for a new baby, above right.

Opposite A gift box is made from two pieces of cardboard, with squares cut from each corner. Fold the sides at right angles and thread ribbon through slots in each edge.

Be inspired by precious black-and-white family photos, baby-blue ribbon, and familiar children's picture books, full of memories.

resources

ANTIQUES

Antique Access
340 North 6th St.
Klamath Falls, OR 97601
541-273-1779
http://www.antiqueaccess.com
Remarkable collection of antiquities and historic ephemera; ivories, marbles, medals, books, and much more.

A Victorian Elegance
Tampa Bay, FL
800-660-3640
http://www.simpleurl.com
A wide selection of vintage and antique clothing, Edwardian, Victorian up to the 1980s, including hats and jewelry.

A Vintage Wedding
An offshoot site of A Victorian Elegance, perfect source for period gifts and inspiration; includes sewing patterns.
http://www.vintagewedding.com

Depot Antique Mall
8313 State Hwy 23
St. Cloud, MN 56301
320-253-6573
http://www.depot-antique-mall.com/

A multi-dealer antique mall in an historic railroad depot; every type of memorabilia.

Elegant Era's
105 Oak Rim Ct #15
Los Gatos, CA 95032
http://www.tias.com/stores/elera/
Fabulous selection of lingerie, lace, silk, linen, jewelry, and more from late 1800s to 1940s.

Ruby Beets Antiques
Poxybogue Road
Bridgehampton, NY 11932
516-537-2802
Painted furniture, old white china, and kitchenware.

Rusty Zipper Vintage Clothing
Portland, OR
503-233-2259
http://www.rustyzipper.com
Incredible online store selling vintage clothing from 1920–1980, including fabrics and sewing patterns.

Tickled Pink Antiques
Internet sales only
888-OLD-STUF
http://www.tias.com
A fine selection of silver, porcelain, pottery, metalware, glass, china, and dinnerware.

Tri-State Antique Center
47 West Pike
Canonsburg, PA 15317
724-745-9116
http://tristateantiques.com
Specializes in Heywood-Wakefield, mid-century modern furniture, and pottery, china, and glass.

A listing of over 40,000 addresses of antiques shops throughout the country exists at http://www.curioscape.com

AUCTIONS

American Pottery Exchange
Internet auctions only
http://www.the-apx.com
Popular ceramics; includes Lu Ray, Russel Wright, Eva Ziesel, McCoy, Bauer, and many more.

Christie's
20 Rockefeller Plaza
New York, NY 10020
212-636-2000
http://www.christies.com
Public auctions in the categories of Contemporary Art, Twentieth-Century Decorative Arts, American Furniture, and Decorative Arts.

EBay
Internet auctions only
http://www.ebay.com
Individual sellers, quality and prices vary, with every category of merchandise represented.

Sotheby's
1334 York Avenue at 72nd Street
New York, NY 10021
212-606-7000
http://www.sothebys.com
Public auctions in Ceramics and Glass, Furniture, and Decorative Arts; also features auctions online.

FABRICS & RIBBONS

Britex Fabrics
146 Geary Street
San Francisco, CA 94108
415-392-2910
http://www.britexfabrics.com
Wide variety of ribbons, trims, and notions.

The Button Emporium & Ribbonry
914 S.W. 11th Avenue
Portland, OR 97205
503-228-6372
http://www.buttonemporium.com
Fine collection of vintage, jacquard, metallic, wired, and assorted ribbons.

Hancock Fabrics
2605A West Main Street
Tupelo, MS 38801
662-844-7368
http://www.hancockfabrics.com
America's largest fabric store, good for all basic decoration needs.

Hyman Hendler and Sons
67 West 38th Street
New York, NY 10018
212-840-8393
http://www.hymanhendler.com
Extensive selection of basic, novelty and vintage ribbons and trims of their own design.

Laura Ashley Home Store
171 East Ridgewood Avenue
Ridgewood, NJ 07450
201-670-0686
http://www.laura-ashleyusa.com
Floral, striped, checked, and solid cottons in a wide variety of colors.

On Board Fabrics
Route 27
P.O. Box 14
Edgecomb, ME 04556
207-882-7536
http://www.onboardfabrics.com
Everything from Balinese cottons to Italian tapestry, botanical prints and woven plaids.

The Ribbon Club
P.O. Box 699
Oregon House, CA 95962
530-692-3014
http://www.theribbonclub.com
Beautiful selection of ribbons, trims, tassels, stamens, and packages for creating flowers.

The Ribbonerie Inc.
191 Potrero Avenue
San Francisco, CA 94103
415-626-6184
http://www.theribbonerie.com
Extensive collection including wired, grosgrain, metallic, and velvet.

Salsa Fabrics
3100 Holly Avenue
Silver Springs, NV 89429
800-758-3819
online store:
http://www.salsafabrics.com
Great original fabrics in cotton, silk, and wool from Guatemala and Indonesia.

Victoria Louise, Mercers
P.O. Box 266
Jefferson, MD 21755
301-473-4949
http://www.fred.net/stull/victoria.html
Fine ribbons, laces, and historical materials.

FLEA MARKETS

Alameda Swap Meet
Located on South Alameda Blvd.
Los Angeles, CA 90021
213-233-2764
Well-known, wide selection, and it never hurts to look; held 7 days a week from 10 a.m. to 7 p.m. year round, 400 vendors.

Brimfield Antique Show
Route 20
Brimfield, MA 01010
413-245-3436
http://www.brimfieldshow.com
Renowned as the outdoor antiques capital of the world, this show is held for a week in the months of May, July, and September.

Denver Indoor Antique Market
1212 South Broadway
Denver, CO 80210
303-744-7049
Wonderful selection; open seven days a week, rain or shine.

Merriam Lane Flea Market
14th and Merriam Lane
Kansas City, KS 66106
913-677-0833
Open air market where estates are bought and sold; operates weekly in spring and summer from 7 a.m. until dark.

Ruth's Flea Market
Highway 431
Roanoke, AL 36274
334-864-7328
With over 300 booths, this market sells all types of collectibles, new and used; held weekly on Wednesdays and Saturdays.

Sullivan Flea Market
Heights Ravenna Road
5 Miles West of Ravenna Center
Ravenna, MI 49451
616-853-2435
Very popular, this flea market is known for its distinct mix of antiques, collectibles, fresh produce, flowers, and consignment; held weekly on Mondays from April to the end of October.

Tesuque Pueblo Flea Market
Route 5
Santa Fe, NM 87501
505-660-8948
This market focuses on Native American Crafts, antiques, rugs, collectibles, and southwest furniture, both new and used; held monthly on Friday–Sunday. Call to verify dates.

Traders Village (Houston)
Eldridge Road
Houston, TX 77083
713-890-5500
Largest marketplace on the Texas Gulf coast, with over 800 dealers and over 60 acres of bargains. Open year-round on Saturday & Sunday, 8 a.m. to 6 p.m.

For listings of flea markets held throughout the country, go to http://www.fleamarketguide.com

INSPIRATION

ABC Carpet & Home
881–888 Broadway
New York, NY 10003
212-674-1144
http://www.abc.home
Exotic collection of home furnishings, fabrics, carpets, and design accessories.

Anthropologie
1700 Sansom Street, 6th Floor
Philadelphia, PA 19103
800-309-2500
http://www.anthropologie.com
Funky, one-of-a-kind items in furniture, hardware, bedding, and drapes.

Kate's Paperie
561 Broadway
New York, NY 10012
212-941-9816
http://www.katespaperie.com
Suppliers of handmade papers, paper goods, and ribbons; their store displays provide creative ideas.

Pier One Imports
1350 North Wells Street
Chicago, IL 60610
312-787-4320
http://www.pier1.com
Home accessories from the Far East, including furniture and outdoor ideas.

Restoration Hardware
The Atrium
300 Boylston Street
Chestnut Hill, MA 02467-1922
617-641-6770
http://www.restorationhardware.com
Not just hardware, but reproduction furnishings for the home or garden.

Takashimaya
693 Fifth Avenue
New York, NY 10012
212-350-0100
Exquisite and exclusive housewares and accessories with an Asian design.

Treillage
418 E 75th Street
New York, NY 10021
212-535-2288
Intriguing garden design shop utilizing architectural details.

PAINTS & PAPERS

Bella Rosa Paper Arts
332 Koski Road
Cloquet, MN 55720
218-879-1134
http://www.bellarosapaperarts.com
Handmade papers, beads, coins, art stamps, fabrics, and collage materials.

Janovic
1150 Third Avenue
New York, NY 10021
800-772-4381
http://www.janovic.com
A quality selection of paints in a wide color range.

Making Tracks Ink
P.O. Box 2045
Bigfork, MT 59911
406-755-6211
http://www.makingtracksink.com
Artistic selection of handmade papers, paints, stamps, embossing powder, cording, and crafting supplies.

Michaels' Arts and Crafts
5959 Alpha Road
Dallas, TX 75240
972-239-2800
http://www.michaels.com
Suppliers of materials for almost any craft with over 470 locations through the country.

NancyJean's
21 Edgewood Dr.
Melbourne, FL 32901
http://www.nancyjeans.com
Wide selection of beautiful craft papers from around the world: India, Japan, Nepal, Germany, Italy and more.

Pearl Paint
3756 Roswell Road
Atlanta, GA 30342
404-233-9400
http://www.pearlpaint.com
Complete supply of materials for arts, crafts, and graphic design.

Ralph Lauren Paint Collection
At Ralph Lauren
867 Madison Avenue
New York, NY 10021
212-606-2100
Signature collection of colors grouped in romantic themes such as River Rock and Desert Hollywood.

The Art Store
600 Martin Luther King Jr. Parkway
Des Moines, Iowa 50312
515-244-7000 or 800-652-2225
Specialty decorating shop for brushes, enamels, varnish, paints, and powders.

Waverly
Dealer locations:
800-423-5881
http://www.waverly.com
Complete supply of decorative accessories including fabric, wallpaper, furniture, window treatments, tabletop, paint, and floor coverings.

We Are Paper
922 N. Noble Street
Chicago, IL 60622
773-486-9374
http://www.wearepaper.com
Colorful supply of 100% recycled cotton papers for any type of project.

Williamsburg Marketplace Catalog
The Colonial Williamsburg Foundation
Department 023
P.O. Box 3532
Williamsburg, VA 23187
800-414-6291
http://www.williamsburgmarketplace.com
Historically accurate home furnishings, prints, and keepsakes.

picture credits

The publisher would like to thank the following for making photography for this book possible:

Annie's
12 Camden Passage
London N1 8ED UK
Tel: (+44) 20 7359 0796
Vintage clothing, accessories, and textiles.

The Button Lady
Hampstead Antique & Craft Emporium
12 Heath Street
London NW3 6TE UK
Tel: (+44) 20 7435 5412 Fax: (+44) 20 8440 5600
Antique and modern buttons, buckles, and hatpins.

Cloud Cuckoo Land
6 Charlton Place
London N1 8AJ UK
Tel: (+44) 20 7354 3141
E. cuckoolandmail@yahoo.co.uk
www.cloudcuckooland.org.uk
Vintage clothing and accessories (1880–1970).

Rosemary Conquest Antiques
4 Charlton Place
London N1 8AJ UK
Tel: (+44) 20 7359 0616
E: rosemary@rosemaryconquest.com
Antiques, chandeliers, and objets d'art.

Eclectica
2 Charlton Place
London N1 8AJ UK
Tel: (+44) 20 7226 5625
E. eclecticaliz@yahoo.co.uk
Vintage costume jewelry and contemporary designer jewelry.

Josephine Ryan Antiques
63 Abbeville Road
London SW4 9JW UK
Tel/Fax: (+44) 20 8675 3900
Antiques, painted furniture, armchairs, glassware, chandeliers.

In addition, the authors and publisher would like to thank the owners of Fife House in Kemptown, Brighton for allowing us to photograph their home.

index

acknowledgments

Thank you to:

Caroline Arber for her beautiful photography and creativity, and to her assistants Ciaran Oliver, Josh Kearns, Etienne Roberts.

Alison Starling who saw the potential in the project and made it possible, and everyone at Ryland Peters and Small, especially Sally Powell and Clare Double.

Maggie Roberts for her valuable contributions to the text; Martin Cassini for his vital contributions to the text and copy editing; Joyce Evans for her exquisite sewing.

All the exhibitors and store owners who were so helpful.

Cathy Madoc Jones, John MacLachlan, and Kathie Conn for the use of vintage items from their private collections; Baśka Dunaj for the hatboxes; Merry Brownfield for her print *Model Backstage*.

For their kind permission to use the following extracts:

The Glass of Fashion by Cecil Beaton: Extracts published by kind permission of The Literary Trustees of Sir Cecil Beaton, Rupert Crew Limited and Weidenfeld & Nicolson.

Encyclopedia of Needlework by Thérèse de Dillmont. DMC Library, Paris. *The Big Book of Needlecraft* edited by Annie S. Paterson. Odhams Press.

The authors have made every effort to secure permission for works in copyright. The publisher will be happy to amend any errors or omissions in future editions.

The following images are courtesy of:

Dorothy Bohm: *Lisbon*, 1954.
Thurston Hopkins: *Couple at party*, 1955. The Getty Images Gallery.
Norman Parkinson: *Pamela Minchin, Jump*, 1939. Norman Parkinson Ltd and Fiona Cowan.
p.72 Donald Silverstein © Vogue, The Condé Nast Publications Ltd.
Chris Ware: *Elizabeth Taylor feeds the pigeons in Trafalgar Square*, 1950. Keystone Collection, The Getty Images Gallery.
Gary Cooper and family on bicycles, Maria Cooper Janis, c/o The Lantz Office, New York.

On a personal note:

A special thankyou to all the friends who helped, especially during the school vacation and while I was on the photographic shoot. Thank you to Martin for everything, to my mother, Joyce, who inspired me, and to my wonderful son, Roman, for his effervescence and good humor throughout.
Jane Cassini

A big "thank you" to my husband, Mick, for his constant love and support, and to Pep, who missed her long walks.
Ann Brownfield